TRIGONOMETRY

MURALILAL C K

Preface

We have tried to make this edition of Trigonometry useful to students in a variety of programs. For example, students who have encountered elements of triangle trig in previous courses may be able to skip all or part of Chapters 1 through 3. Students preparing for technical courses may not need much of the material after Chapter 6 or 7. Chapters 9 and 10 cover vectors and polar coordinates, optional topics that occur in some trigonometry courses but are often reserved for precalculus.

There are many reasons why students might find trigonometry difficult, among them:

- The subject inherently involves a great deal of technical detail, which can be allowed to obscure the main ideas.
- The subject is often taught with the analytical rigor appropriate to a precalculus course -- before students have acquired the necessary facility with functions.

In his beautiful book, Trigonometric Delights, Eli Maor enjoins us "Let's not forget that trigonometry is, first and foremost, a practical discipline, born out of and deeply rooted in applications." After the New Math "[f]ormal definitions and legalistic verbosity—all in the name of mathematical rigor—replaced a real understanding of the subject." And formalism is "... certainly not the best way to motivate the beginning student."

Contents

Foreword

" may well be greeted with panic and bewilderment. So we do not begin with a preliminary chapter covering all the mathematical topics needed for the rest of the course, including elements of analytic geometry and properties of functions such as domain and range, symmetry, transformations, composition, and inverse functions. (This material usually comprises most of a precalculus course, which is usually taught after trigonometry, where it is introduced using more familiar, hence easier, functions as examples.)

Nor do we begin with a chapter about angles, including coterminal and reference angles, converting degrees to minutes and seconds, radians, arc length, and angular velocity, before the trig ratios are even mentioned. We have tried to address these issues as follows:

• Chapter 1 reviews only the most basic facts about triangles and circles that students will need to begin their study of trigonometry, and may be omitted or assigned as homework. Other facts about functions and angles are introduced when they are needed. For example, minutes and seconds are discussed in the context of parallax in the section on Law of Sines in Chapter 3. Nautical bearings occur in Section 4.1, Angles and Rotation.

• Chapter 2 introduces the three (not six) basic trig ratios, and considers angles in the first quadrant only. We believe this initial simplicity allows students to focus on the fundamental concepts without simultaneously trying to master a welter of peripheral detail.

• In Chapter 3 we introduce reference angles for the second quadrant in order to study obtuse triangles and the Laws of Sines and Cosines. Reference angles are covered again in more generality in Chapter 4.

Preface

Preface

We have tried to make this edition of Trigonometry useful to students in a variety of programs. For example, students who have encountered elements of triangle trig in previous courses may be able to skip all or part of Chapters 1 through 3. Students preparing for technical courses may not need much of the material after Chapter 6 or 7. Chapters 9 and 10 cover vectors and polar coordinates, optional topics that occur in some trigonometry courses but are often reserved for precalculus.

There are many reasons why students might find trigonometry difficult, among them:

• The subject inherently involves a great deal of technical detail, which can be allowed to obscure the main ideas.

• The subject is often taught with the analytical rigor appropriate to a precalculus course -- before students have acquired the necessary facility with functions.

In his beautiful book, Trigonometric Delights, Eli Maor enjoins us "Let's not forget that trigonometry is, first and foremost, a practical discipline, born out of and deeply rooted in applications." After the New Math "[f]ormal definitions and legalistic verbosity—all in the name of mathematical rigor—replaced a real understanding of the subject." And formalism is "... certainly not the best way to motivate the beginning student."

" may well be greeted with panic and bewilderment. So we do not begin with a preliminary chapter covering all the mathematical topics needed for the rest of the course, including elements of analytic geometry and properties of functions such as domain and range, symmetry, transformations, composition, and inverse functions. (This material usually comprises most of a precalculus course, which is usually taught after trigonometry, where it is introduced using more familiar, hence easier, functions as examples.)

Nor do we begin with a chapter about angles, including coterminal and reference angles, converting degrees to minutes and seconds, radians, arc length, and angular velocity, before the trig ratios are even mentioned. We have tried to address these issues as follows:

• Chapter 1 reviews only the most basic facts about triangles and circles that students will need to begin their study of trigonometry, and may be omitted or assigned as homework. Other facts about functions and angles are introduced when they are needed. For example, minutes and seconds are discussed in the context of parallax in the section on Law of Sines in Chapter 3. Nautical bearings occur in Section 4.1, Angles and Rotation.

• Chapter 2 introduces the three (not six) basic trig ratios, and considers angles in the first quadrant only. We believe this initial simplicity allows students to focus on the fundamental concepts without simultaneously trying to master a welter of peripheral detail.

• In Chapter 3 we introduce reference angles for the second quadrant in order to study obtuse triangles and the Laws of Sines and Cosines. Reference angles are covered again in more generality in Chapter 4.

v

vi

• Chapter 4 considers angles as rotations in preparation for the graphs of sine and cosine. Note that the applications of periodic functions in this chapter are functions of degrees only, to fit with our approach: radians come later, after students have some experience with sinusoidal graphs.

• Chapter 5 begins with a section on algebraic manipulations with trig ratios, a skill that is often neglected but can engender endless confusion for students. This chapter treats only simple equations and identities; more equations and identities appear in Chapters 7 and 8. We solve equations both graphically and analytically, and we use graphs as well as algebra to verify trigonometric identities.

- Chapter 6 introduces radians and the circular functions of real numbers. Most of this chapter and Chapter 7 revisit basic skills such as analyzing graphs and solving equations, but working now in radians rather than degrees.
- Chapter 8 studies identities and their use in more detail, including the sum and difference formulas and the double angle identities. Inverse trig functions are included here, and are the three reciprocal trig functions.
- Chapters 9 and 10 cover ancillary topics; typical trigonometry courses may include one or more of these topics: vectors, polar coordinates, and complex numbers.

In addition to the Homework Problems, each Example in the book is followed by a similar Exercise for students to test their understanding. Each Section concludes with a Summary , a set of Study Questions, and a list of Skills to be addressed in the Homework. A Summary and a set of Review Problems follows each chapter. Chapters 1 through 8 include Activities for students to work through some of the main ideas. We have described the use of a graphing calculator, but other graphing utilities can easily be substituted.

Throughout we have been guided by the Rule of Four and use tables and graphical representation to illustrate concepts. We have taken care to include numerical examples and diagrams, both in Examples and in Homework Problems, to offer students some intuitive understanding for the more abstract ideas of trigonometry. Above all, we have tried to focus on the fundamental ideas of trigonometry by introducing them in their most basic form and returning later to look at them in greater detail.

CHAPTER ONE

Contents

Preface v

1 Triangles and Circles 1

1.1 Angles and Triangles 3

Triangles. 4

Angles 6

Section 1.1 Summary 9

Homework 1.1 10

1.2 Similar Triangles 15

Congruent Triangles 15

Similar Triangles 16

Using Proportions with Similar Triangles 18

Similar Right Triangles 19

Overlapping Triangles 20

Section 1.2 Summary 21

Homework 1.2 22

1.3 Circles 27

The Distance Formula 27

Equation for a Circle 29

Rational and Irrational Numbers 30

Circumference and Area 31

Section 1.3 Summary 33

Homework 1.3 34

1.4 Chapter 1 Summary and Review 40

Key Concepts 40

Chapter 1 Review Problems 41

2 The Trigonometric Ratios 47
2.1 Side and Angle Relationships 51
Introduction 51
The Triangle Inequality 52
Right Triangles: The Pythagorean Theorem 52
Section 2.1 Summary 54
Homework 2.1 55

2.2 Right Triangle Trigonometry. 58
The Sine of an Angle 59
Using a Calculator 60
Using the Sine Ratio to Find an Unknown Side. 61
The Cosine and the Tangent 62
The Three Trigonometric Ratios 65
Section 2.2 Summary 67
Homework 2.2 68
2.3 Solving Right Triangles. 73
Introduction 73
Finding an Angle 74
The Special Angles 76
The Trigonometric Ratios for the Special Angles 77
Section 2.3 Summary 79
Homework 2.3 80
2.4 Chapter 2 Summary and Review 84
Key Concepts 84
Chapter 2 Review Problems 86

3 Laws of Sines and Cosines 91
3.1 Obtuse Angles 92
Angles in Standard Position. 92
Trigonometric Ratios for Obtuse Angles 95
Using a Calculator 96
Trigonometric Ratios for Supplementary Angles 97
Supplements of the Special Angles 99
The Area of a Triangle 100
Section 3.1 Summary 102
Homework 3.1 104
3.2 The Law of Sines 110
Finding a Side. 111
Solving Triangles with the Law of Sines 112
Finding an Angle 113
Applications 115
Measuring Astronomical Distances 116
Small Angles: Minutes and Seconds 117
Section 3.2 Summary 119

Homework 3.2 120
3.3 The Law of Cosines 125
Finding a Side. 126
Finding an Angle 127
Using the Law of Cosines for the Ambiguous Case. 128
Navigation 130
Which Law to Use 132
Section 3.3 Summary 133
Homework 3.3 134
3.4 Chapter 3 Summary and Review 139
Key Concepts 139
Chapter 3 Review Problems 141
3.5 Chapter 3 Activity 146

4 Trigonometric Functions 151
4.1 Angles and Rotation. 153
Introduction 153
Angles in Standard Position. 153
Trigonometric Ratios for All Angles 155
Reference Angles 157
Using Reference Angles 160
Coterminal Angles 162
Solving Trigonometric Equations 163
The Special Angles 165
The Unit Circle 168
Section 4.1 Summary 170
Homework 4.1 172
4.2 Graphs of Trigonometric Functions 176
Location by Coordinates 176
Bearings 177
A Periodic Function of Angle 178
The Sine Function 179
The Cosine Function 181
Function Notation 183
The Tangent Function 185
Angle of Inclination 187
Section 4.2 Summary 189
Homework 4.2 191
4.3 Periodic Functions 199
Period, Midline and Amplitude 199
Sinusoidal Functions 202
Other Periodic Functions 204
Section 4.3 Summary 207
Homework 4.3 208
4.4 Chapter 4 Summary and Review 220
Key Concepts 220

Chapter 4 Review Problems 223
5 Equations and Identities 227
5.1 Algebra with Trigonometric Ratios 229
Evaluating Trigonometric Expressions 229
Simplifying Trigonometric Expressions 230
Powers of Trigonometric Ratios 232
Products. 232
Factoring 233
Section 5.1 Summary 235
Homework 5.1 236
5.2 Solving Equations. 238
Introduction 238
Trigonometric Equations 239
Solving Trigonometric Equations 240
Graphical Solutions 243
Equations with Squares of Trig Ratios 244
Snell's Law 246
Section 5.2 Summary 247
Homework 5.2 248

5.3 Trigonometric Identities 250
What is an Identity? 250
Using Trigonometric Ratios in Identities 251
Checking Identities Graphically 252
Pythagorean Identity 253
Tangent Identity 255
Trig Ratios are Related 256
Solving Equations 257
Proving Identities 258
Section 5.3 Summary 259
Homework 5.3 261
5.4 Chapter 5 Summary and Review 263
Key Concepts 263
Chapter 5 Review Problems 264
6 Radians 269
6.1 Arclength and Radians 271
Arclength 272
Measuring Angles in Radians 273
Converting Between Degrees and Radians. 275
Arclength Formula 276
Unit Circle 277
Section 6.1 Summary 278
Homework 6.1 280
6.2 The Circular Functions 284
Trigonometric Functions of Angles in Radians 284
The Special Values 286

Sine and Cosine of Real Numbers 288
Coordinates on a Unit Circle 290
The Tangent Function 291
Section 6.2 Summary 293
Homework 6.2 295
6.3 Graphs of the Circular Functions 301
The Sine and Cosine Functions 301
The Tangent Function 304
Solving Equations 306
Modeling with Circular Functions. 307
Domain and Range 309
Section 6.3 Summary 311
Homework 6.3 313
6.4 Chapter 6 Summary and Review 322
Key Concepts 322
Chapter 6 Review Problems 324
7 Circular Functions 329
7.1 Transformations of Graphs 331
Period, Midline, and Amplitude 331
Graphs of Sinusoidal Functions 334
Modeling with Sinusoidal Functions 335
The Tangent Function 337
Section 7.1 Summary 338
Homework 7-1. 340

7.2 The General Sinusoidal Function 346
Horizontal Shifts 346
Combining Transformations 349
Modeling with Sinusoidal Functions 353
Section 7.2 Summary 356
Homework 7-2. 357
7.3 Solving Equations. 367
Introduction 367
Multiple Solutions 371
Using a Calculator for Multiple Solutions 372
Using a Substitution 373
Applications 375
Section 7.3 Summary 377
Homework 7-3. 378
7.4 Chapter 7 Summary and Review 380
Key Concepts 380
Review Problems. 382
8 More Functions and Identities 387
8.1 Sum and Difference Formulas 389
The Sum of Angles Identities 389
The Difference of Angles Identities 392

Sum and Difference Identities for Tangent. 393
Double Angle Identities 394
Solving Equations 396
Section 8.1 Summary 398
Homework 8-1. 399
8.2 Inverse Trigonometric Functions 404
Inverse of a Function 404
The Graph of the Inverse 406
Does Every Function Have an Inverse? 407
Restricting the Domain: The Inverse Sine Function 409
The Inverse Cosine and Inverse Tangent Functions 411
Modeling with Inverse Functions 414
Alternate Notations. 414
Simplifying Expressions 415
Section 8.2 Summary 417
Homework 8-2. 419
8.3 The Reciprocal Functions 425
Three More Functions 425
Application to Right Triangles 427
Graphs of the Reciprocal Functions 428
Solving Equations 430
Using Identities 430
Section 8.3 Summary 434
Homework 8-3. 436
8.4 Chapter Summary and Review 442
Key Concepts 442
Review Problems. 445

9 Vectors 451
9.1 Geometric Form 453
Introduction 453
Notation for Vectors 454
Scalar Multiplication of Vectors 455
Addition of Vectors 456
Velocity 459
Components of a Vector 461
Using Components 462
Section 9.1 Summary 464
Homework 9-1. 465
9.2 Coordinate Form 469
Introduction 469
Unit Vectors 470
Converting Between Geometric and Coordinate Form 471
Scalar Multiples of Vectors in Coordinate Form. 472
Adding Vectors in Coordinate Form 473
Force 476

Section 9.2 Summary 478
Homework 9-2. 480
9.3 The Dot Product 483
Components 483
Coordinate Form for Components. 484
The Dot Product. 486
Geometric Meaning of the Dot Product 487
Section 9.3 Summary 490
Homework 9-3. 491
9.4 Chapter Summary and Review 494
Key Concepts 494
Review Problems. 496
10 Polar Coordinates and Complex Numbers 499
10.1 Polar Coordinates. 501
Plotting Points 503
Regions in the Plane 504
Converting Between Polar and Cartesian Coordinates 506
Equations in Polar Coordinates 508
Section 10.1 Summary 509
Homework 10-1 511
10.2 Polar Graphs 513
Graphing in Polar Coordinates. 513
Using a Graphing Calculator 515
Sketching Familiar Equations 517
Finding Intersection Points 520
A Catalog of Polar Curves 522
Section 10.2 Summary 523
Homework 10-2 524

10.3 Complex Numbers 530
Imaginary Numbers. 530
Complex Numbers 531
Arithmetic of Complex Numbers 532
Products of Complex Numbers. 533
Quotients of Complex Numbers 534
Graphing Complex Numbers 536
Zeros of Polynomials 538
Section 10.3 Summary 541
Homework 10-3 543
10.4 Polar Form for Complex Numbers 545
Introduction 545
Polar Form 546
Products and Quotients in Polar Form 547
Powers and Roots of Complex Numbers 549
Section 10.4 Summary 551
Homework 10-4 553

Index

z, see complex conjugate
, 31
acos, see also inverse cosine, 414
acute angle, 6
addition formula, see also sum of angles, 394
algebraic expression, see also expression, 229
alternate interior angles, 8
altitude
of a triangle, 15
ambiguous case, 114, 128
amplitude, 180
angle, 3, 6
acute, see also acute angle, 6
alternate interior, see also alternate
interior angles, 8
as rotation, 153
central, 13
complementary, see also complementary
angles, 6
corresponding, see also corresponding
angles, 8
coterminal, 162
exterior, 11
find, 74, 113, 127
in radians, see also radian, 273
inscribed, 13
obtuse, see also obtuse angle, 6, 92
of incidence, 246
of refraction, 246
reference, 157, see also reference angle
right, 3
special, 76, 77
standard position, 92, 153
straight, 3
supplementary, see also supplementary
angles, 6, 99
vertical, see also vertical angles, 7
angle of inclination, 187
arccos, see also inverse cosine, 414
arclength, 31, 271, 272
formula, 276
arcsin, see also inverse sine, 414
arctan, see also inverse tangent, 414
area

of triangle, 100
asin, see also inverse sine, 414
astronomical unit (AU), 117
atan, see also inverse tangent, 414
bearing, 177
center, 29
circle, 29
circumscribing, 147
equation, 29
circular function, see also cosine, see also
sine, 290
circumference, 31
complementary angles, 6
complex conjugate, 535
complex number, 530
graphing, 536
length, see also modulus, 536
quotient of, 534
complex plane, 536
component, see also vector, 461, 483
coordinate form, 484
vector component, 485
conclusion, 3
congruent triangles, 15
conjugate, see also complex conjugate, 534
converse, 3
conversions equations, 508
corresponding angles, 8
cos ?1, see also inverse trigonometric
function, 75, 411
cosecant, 425
cosine, 62
of a real number, 288
cosine function, see also cosine, 181
cosine ratio, 62
685
686 INDEX
cotangent, 425
coterminal angles, 162
difference of angles, 393
discriminant, 129
distance formula, 27
domain, 309
restrict, 409
dot product, 486
geometric form, 487
double angle formulas, see also double angle
identity, 394

double angle identity, 394
equation, 238
conditional, 250
trigonometric, see also trigonometric
equation, 239
equilateral triangle, 5
equilibrium, 477
equivalent, 230
evaluate, 229
expression, 229
trigonometric, see also trigonometric
expression, 229
FOIL (acronym: First, Outside, Inside, Last),
233
force, 476
function
notation, 183
sinusoidal, 202
Greek alphabet, 9
hypotenuse, 16, 52
hypothesis, 3
identity, 250
check graphically, 252
proving, 258
Pythagorean, see also Pythagorean
identity, 253
with trigonometric ratios, see also
trigonometric identity, 251
imaginary
axis, 536
number, 530
imginary part, 532
initial side of an angle in standard position,
92
input variable, 178, 183
inverse
function, see also inverse trigonometric
function, 404, 405, 408
graph of, 406
operation, see also inverse, 404
inverse cosine, 411
inverse sine, 410
inverse tangent, 412
inverse trigonometric function, 75, 404
irrational number, 30
isosceles triangle, 6
law of cosines, 125
law of sines, 110, 146

leg, 16, 52
Lissajous figure, 151
loudness, 329
magnitude of a vector, 454
mathematical model, 178
Mercator map, 387
and secant function, 388
midline, 180
modulus, 536
normal line, 246
oblique triangle, 92, 119, 131
obtuse angle, 6, 94
one-to-one, 408
opposite vector, 477
orthogonal, 488
output variable, 178, 183
parallax, 116
parallelogram rule, 458
parameter, 201
parsec, 118
period, 180
periodic function, 178, 180, 199, 204
pitch of musical note, 329
polar axis, 502
polar coordinates, 502
converting Cartesian, 506
equations, 508
graphing, 513
polar form, 545, 546
polar graphs, 513
catalog of curves, 522
pole, 502
polygon
regular, 12
pure imaginary number, see also imaginary
number, 532
Pythagorean identity, 253
Pythagorean theorem, 52, 58, 126
converse, 53
687
quadrantal angles, 99
radian, 270, 271, 273
radius, 29
range, 310
rational number, 30
real axis, 536
real part, 532
reciprocal function, see also cosecant, see also

cotangent, see also secant, 425, 433
graph, 428
reciprocal ratio, see also reciprocal function,
433
rectangular coordinate system, 501
reference angle, 157, 158, 160
reference triangle, 157
repeating decimal, see also rational number,
30
resultant force, 476
right angle, 3
right triangle
Pythagorean theorem, 52
similar, 18
solving, 73, 131
trigonometry, 58
rotation, 153, 163
scalar, 454
multiplication, 455
scalar product, see also dot product, 486
scalene triangle, 10
secant, 425
Mercator map, 388
sector, 32
self-similarity, 500
similar triangles, 15, 16
proportions, 18
right triangles, 18
simplify, 230
sin , see also sine, 59
sin ?1, see also inverse trigonometric
function, 75, 410
sine, 59
of a real number, 288
of an acute angle, 59
using to find an unknown side, 61
sine function, see also sine, 179
sine ratio, see also sine, 61
sinusoidal function, 202
graph, 334
slope, 187
Snell's Law, 246
solve
a triangle, 73
an equation, 238
an equation using a graph, 239
inequality, 52
right triangle, 73

trigonometric equations, see also
trigonometric equation, 240
special angles, 165
radians, 286
supplements of, 99
straight angle, 3
substitution
to solve trigonometric equations, 373
subtend, 147
sum of angles, 393
supplementary angles, 6
trigonometric ratios of, 97
tan , see also tangent, 62
tan ?1, see also inverse trigonometric
function, 75, 412
tangent, 62
tangent function, see also tangent, 185, 291,
337
tangent identity, 255
tangent ratio, 62
terminal side of an angle in standard
position, 93
terminating decimal, see also rational
number, 30
timbre, 329
transformation, 331
combining, 349
triangle, 3, 4
altitude, 15
area of, 100
equilateral, see also equilateral triangle,
5
exterior angle, 11
isosceles, see also isosceles triangle, 6
oblique, 92, see also oblique triangle
overlapping, 19
reference, 157
scalene, 10
similar, see also similar triangles, 16
solving, 131
triangle inequality, 52
triangulation, 47
trigonometric equation, 157, 163, 239
graphical solutions, 243
solving, 240, 257, 367, 430
with squares of trig ratios, 244
trigonometric expression, 229
factoring, 233

simplifying, 230
688 INDEX
trigonometric function, see also trigonometric
ratios, 151
graph, 176
product of, 232
raising to power, 232
trigonometric identity, 251, 430
double angle, 394
sum and difference for tangent, 393
sum of angles, 389
trigonometric ratios
for all angles, 155
obtuse angle, 94, 95
supplementary angles, 97
trigonometry
right triangle, 58
unit circle, 30, 166, 168
arclength and radians, 277
vector, 451, 453
adding, 473
component, 485
coordinate form, 469
displacement, 456
geometric vs coordinate form, 471
notation, 454
opposite, 477
position, 453
resultant, 457
unit, 470
zero, 477
velocity, 459
vertex angle
of an isosceles triangle, 6
vertical angles, 7
zero of a polynomial, 538
zero vector, 477

Printed by Libri Plureos GmbH in Hamburg,
Germany